I0504761

# Confidence on Video Creation: Make professional videos, easily

IRUKA CHINEMEREM MBARIKATTA

Copyright © 2020 Iruka Chinemerem Mbarikatta

All rights reserved.

ISBN:

# DEDICATION

I dedicate this book to great entrepreneurs who in one way or the other find it difficult to create professional content videos either for themselves or other persons business

# TABLE OF CONTENTS

# INTRODUCTION

In this age of digital marketing, video is also one of the best means for promoting yourself, your business, or products/services.

This eBook shares useful tips to help you create professional content videos that are capable of generating millions of views and snatching easy front page rankings.

Want to know how to create professional content videos that are capable of generating millions of views and snatching easy front page rankings? If so, you need to check out this new video system called "Content Samurai"... https://www.contentsamurai.com/c/iruka-cs-freetrial Don't be in a hurry!

Relax you will get value reading all through.

I guarantee you've never seen anything like this before… Mark my words, it's going to completely change the way you do digital marketing forever.

Why? As you know video is now critical for just about every aspect of digital marketing today… However, because creating videos has always been a laborious, expensive and highly technical process, in the past it's really only been available to big businesses with BIG budgets.

But finally that's all changed… Because Content Samurai's revolutionary new video creation system is SO EASY to use, generating tons of professional videos that produce an avalanche of traffic is now anyone's game…

And it's fast, REALLY FAST… So, if you want the ultimate shortcut to start killing it with video, do yourself a favour and check out Content Samurai now…

And best of all, it's free to get started! You can get free access here:

This software is the fastest way to create quality content.

This is first intelligent video creator that does all the hard work for you.

It helps you create a professional video content in just 10 sec.

With a push of a button content samurai reviews, your script cuts it up into professional slide layout and formats your text. The bones of your video are formed in seconds.

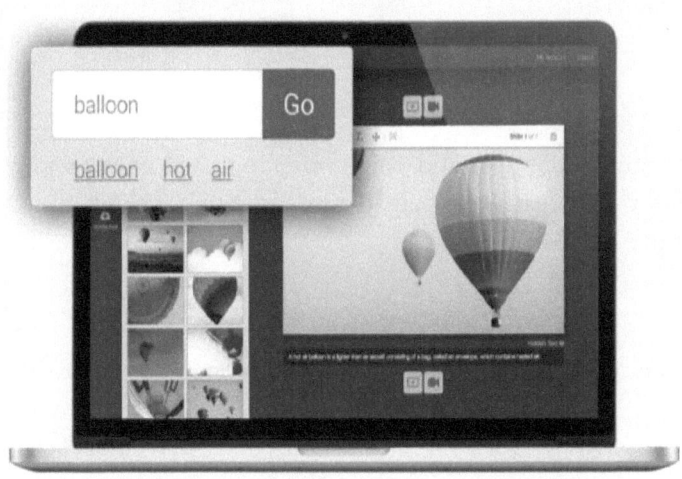

Content samurai analyses your script and intelligently suggests the perfect images for your video from a library of over 112 million quality images.

It's powered by cutting edge text and voice matching tech. content samurai automatically edits your video from beginning to end with a single click. It's video creation at the speed of thought.

**So let's get started.** You can do this either with your Smartphone or Pc.

➢ First of all , click on this link https://www.contentsamurai.com/c/iruka-cs-freetrial
➢ Click on free trial
➢ Enter your name and email address (best is to use Gmail account)

After entering correct name and email address, you will receive mail to set up your password.

Scroll down, you will see **set up a password**. Enter your preferable password and confirm the password. Ensure you accept their terms and condition by clicking on the agree button.

Once this is done, it takes you straight to the main page. It will display Create a new video

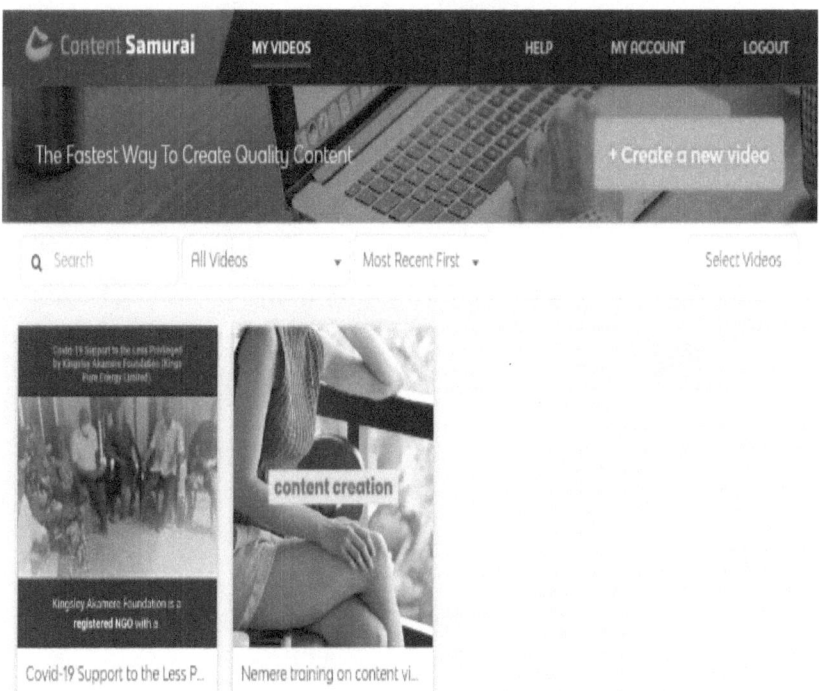

Here are the tools you will see: My videos, Help, My account, Logout on the top bar while Template, script, scenes, voice, preview and download is at the left bar.

Don't be confused just with a space of 10 -20 minutes you will be familiar with all the tools.

Let's explain each tool for easier understanding.

# HOW TO USE TEMPLATE FOR YOUR CONTENT

This tool enables you to select the best format that's in line with the kind of video content you want to create. Example: content video, influencer video, instant ad, sales video, course/training video, property listing, my custom templates.

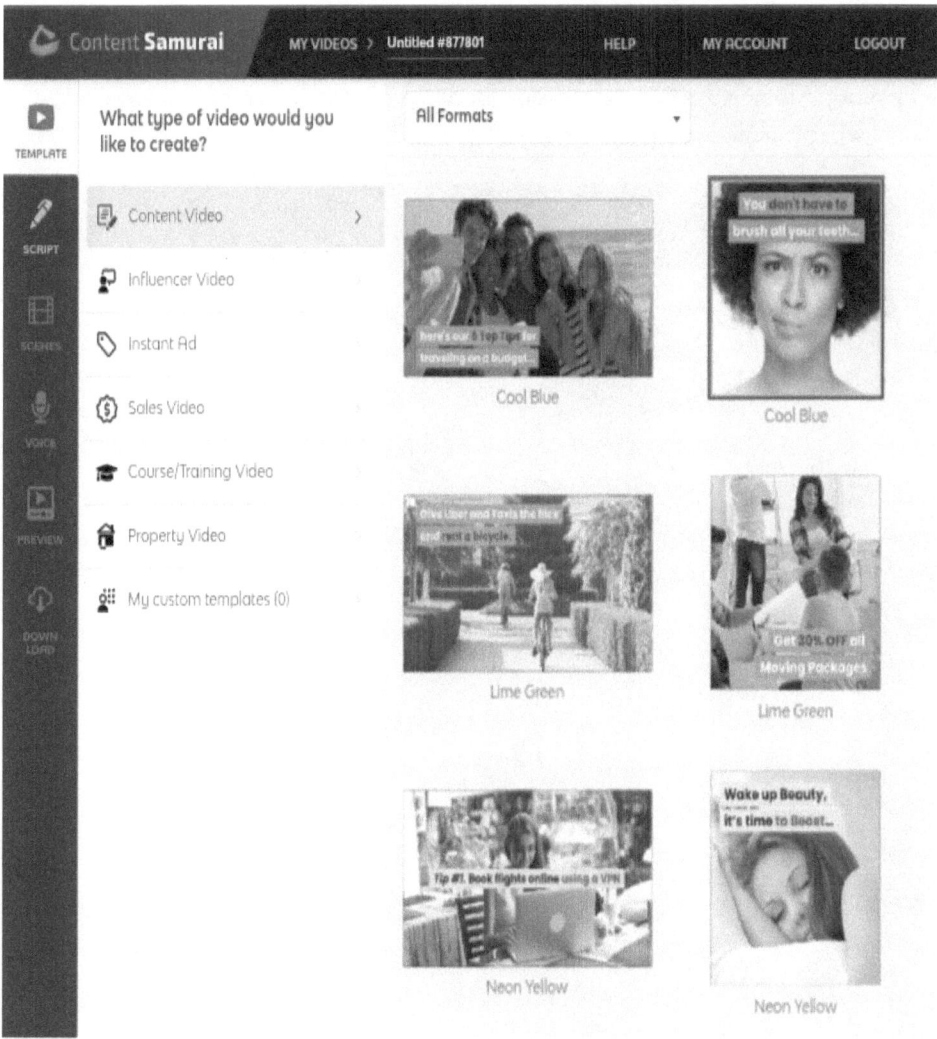

You can choose from any of the listed template above that's related to the content you want to use in creating the video. Click ok to use.

**N: B.** Always have your write up down, it helps you to choose the best template.

## HOW TO USE SCRIPT TO CREATE VIDEOS IN SECONDS

This is where you type in your content for automatic scenes generation. Ensure you type words correctly. Make use of question mark (?), colon (:), semicolon, coma etc, where necessary because automatic voice reader reads exactly what is generated from your script.

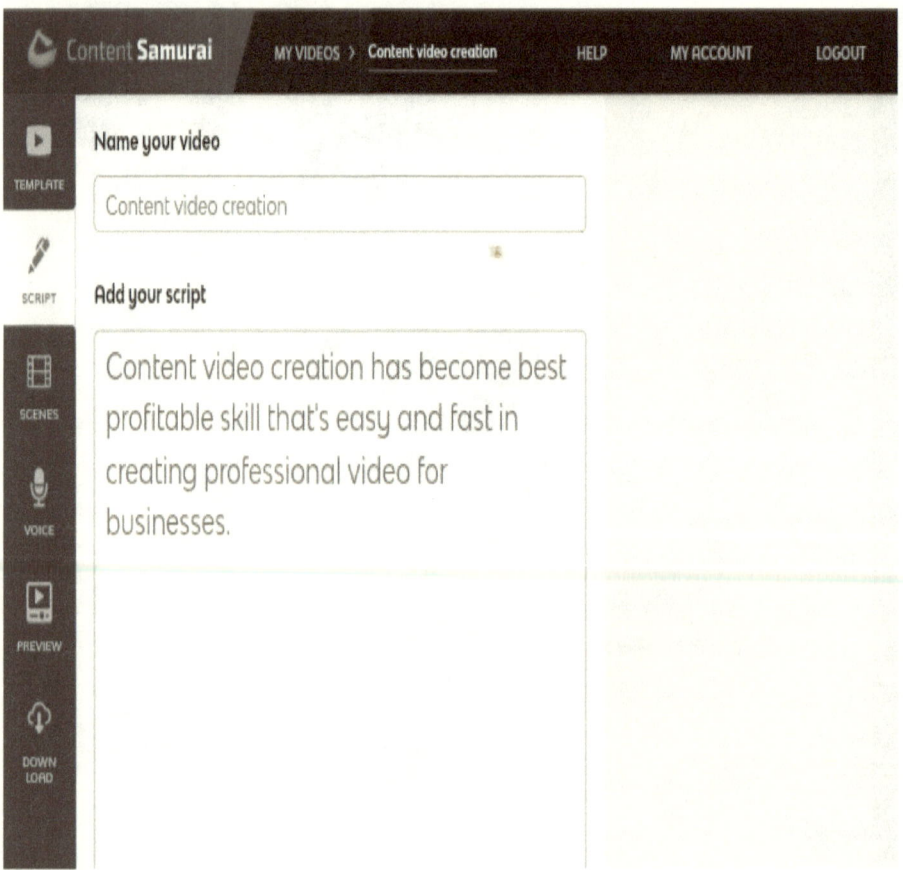

After typing your content, click on create scenes.

**Note,** once you click on create scene you cannot edit the script again unless through scene tool.

However, you make necessary corrections on script before proceeding to create your scene.

## CONVERTING YOUR SCRIPT INTO SCENES

Here is where your creativity is highly needed…ensure you choose images or video clip that best explains your content in each scene.

Scene has sub-tools like;

- ❖ media

- ❖ layout

- ❖ styles

- ❖ **Find media**: this is used when you prefer photos or video clips in content samurai.

- ❖ **Upload**: this is when you upload your photo/video from your Smartphone or PC.

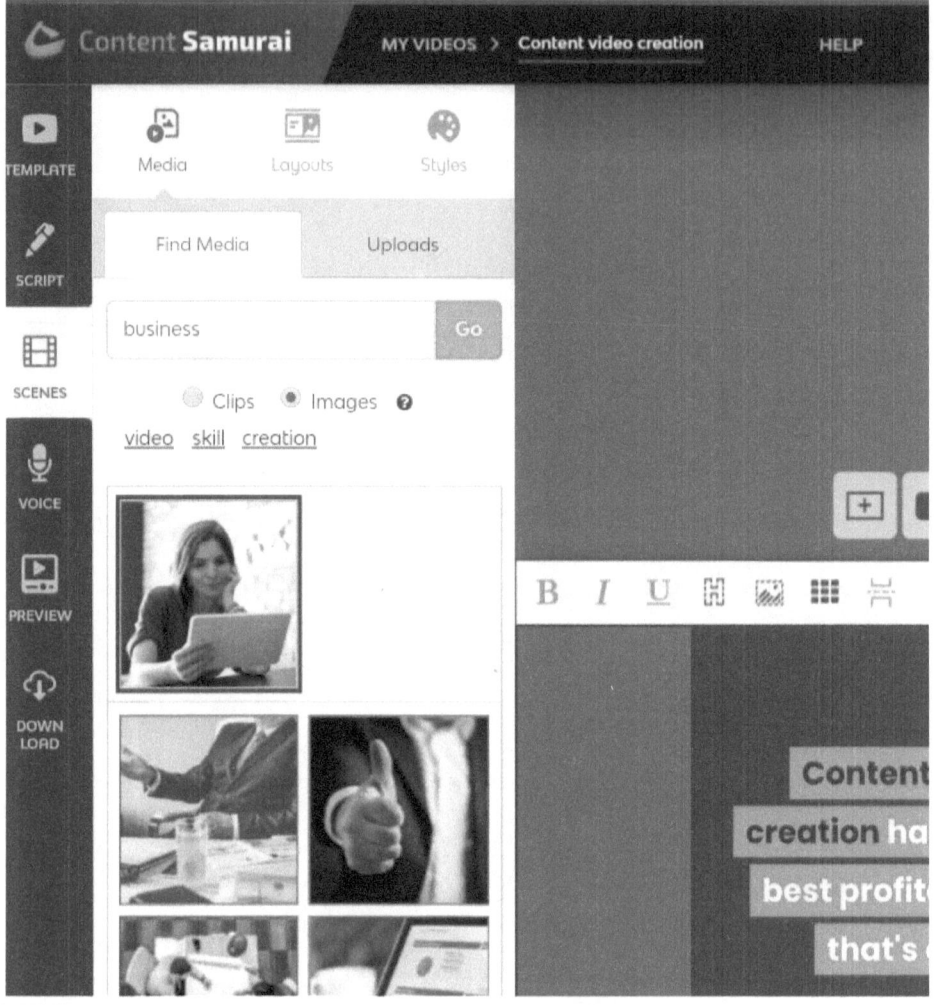

Everything needed to create a professional video is already in content samurai, so make it count.

Note: you can as well change the layout or styles but I will advice you leave the way it appears.

## ADDING VOICE TRACK

This is the tool that reads the text for audience.  It contains:

- ✓ No voice-track (music only) – that's use your video without voiceover or auto-voice.
- ✓ Auto-voice: It's automatic voice that reads your text either in a male/female voice depending on your preferable country.
- ✓ Record your voice track: you can use this by clicking on it. Then you start recording or by uploading a voice track related to your content.

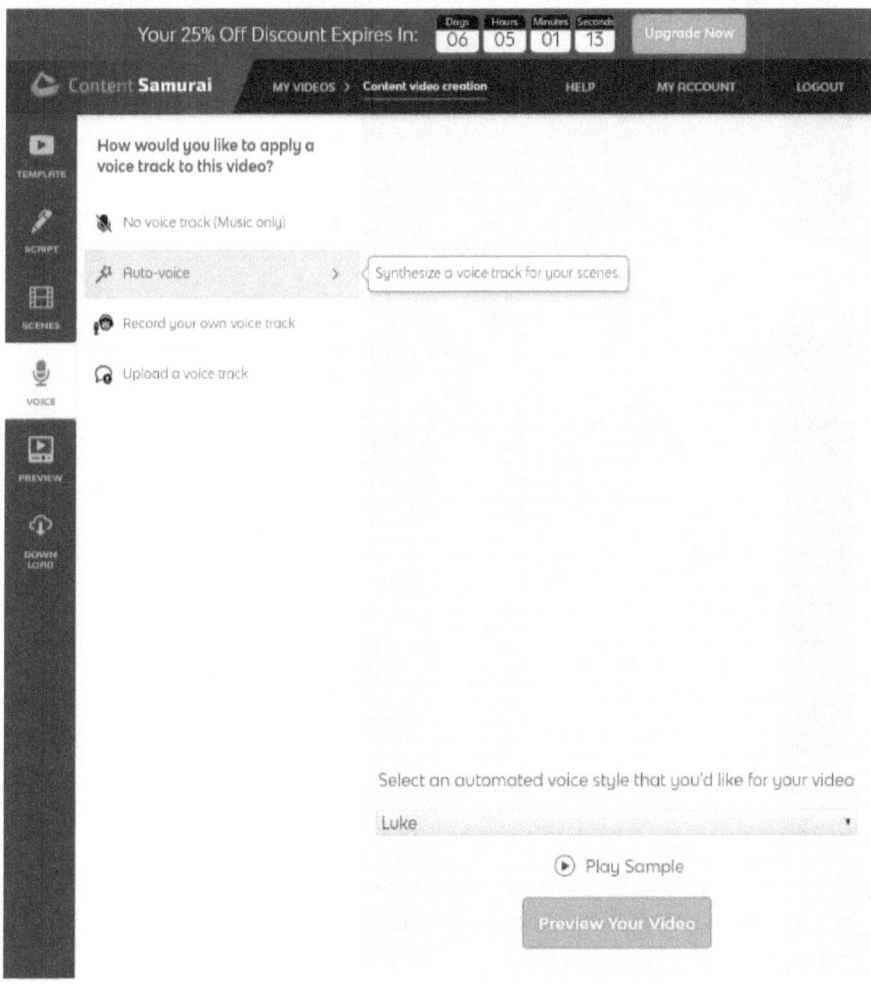

After selecting your preferable voice then click on preview your video.

## HOW TO PREVIEW AND ADD MUSIC BACKGROUND

This tool helps you select music, adjust the music volume and voice track speed. Ensure you select the best mood and genre that suits your content video.

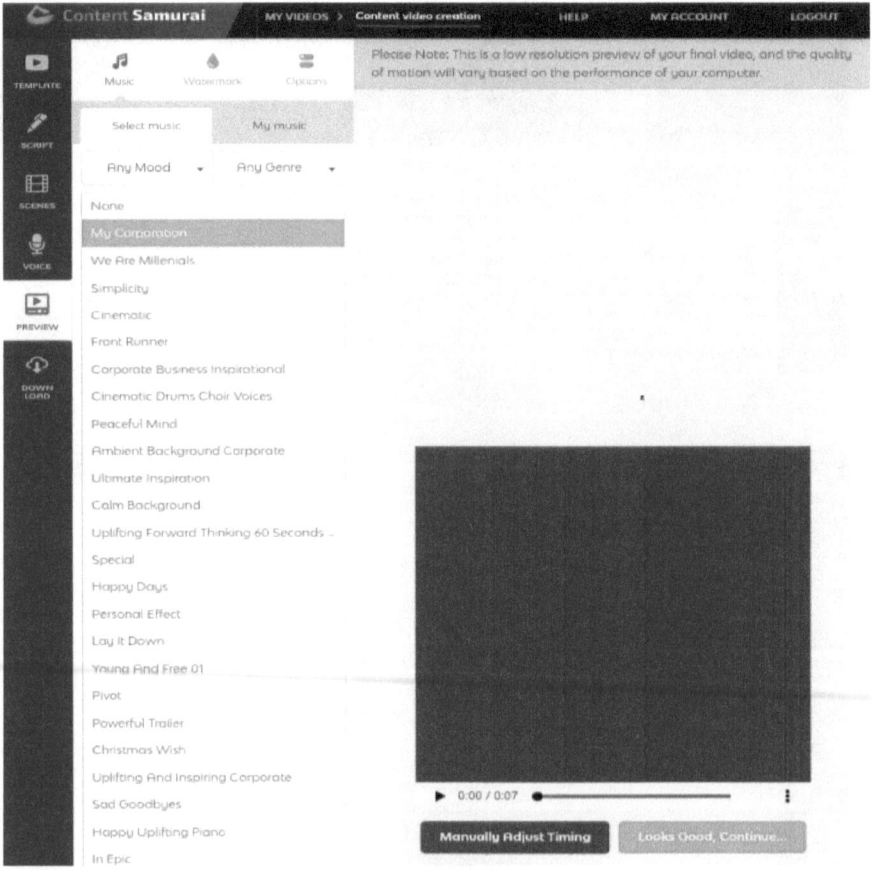

Replay the video again after selecting background music. Adjust also voice speed and music volume by clicking on option. If it looks good to you, click on download

## DOWNLOAD

This tool generates your video for everyone to be able to watch or view it.

First click on download, allow it to display generate video then click on generate your video, remain on the page for the process to complete.

Then click on download now. Your video is ready for use.

Click on this link to get started: https://www.contentsamurai.com/c/iruka-cs-freetrial

*Interesting right!*

*Make out time to practice what you have learnt and don't keep calm.*

**Make noise let people know what you can do and monetize your skill.**

*Remember, the only thing that can stop you from achieving your goal is "you". Take action don't procrastinate because it kills dreams*

## ABOUT THE AUTHOR

Nemere is a content video creator expert, graphic designer, sales and network marketing consultant and trainer.

Her network marketing has affected more than 500 lives directly and indirectly. She had created more than 150 content videos for different clients in less than 6 months which had been acknowledged by clients to be super-catchy and amazing.

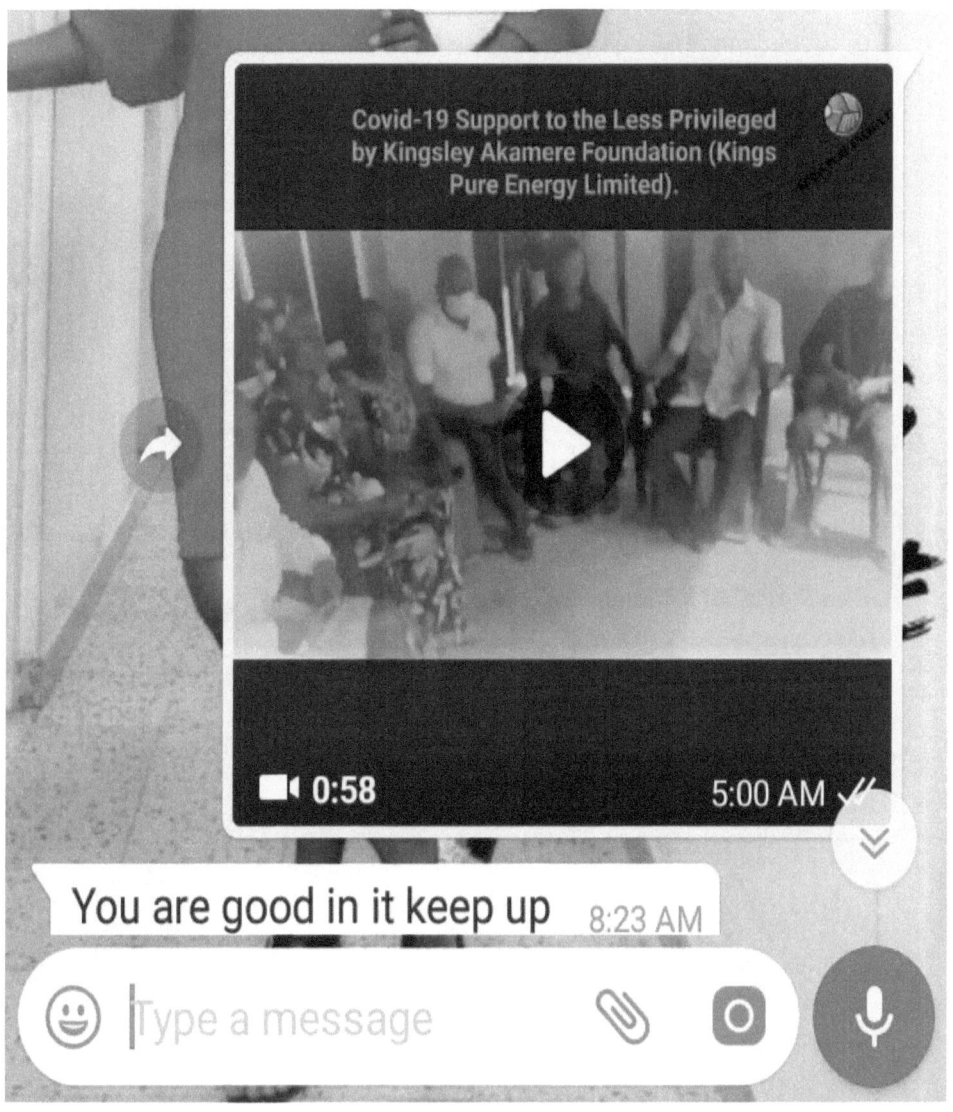

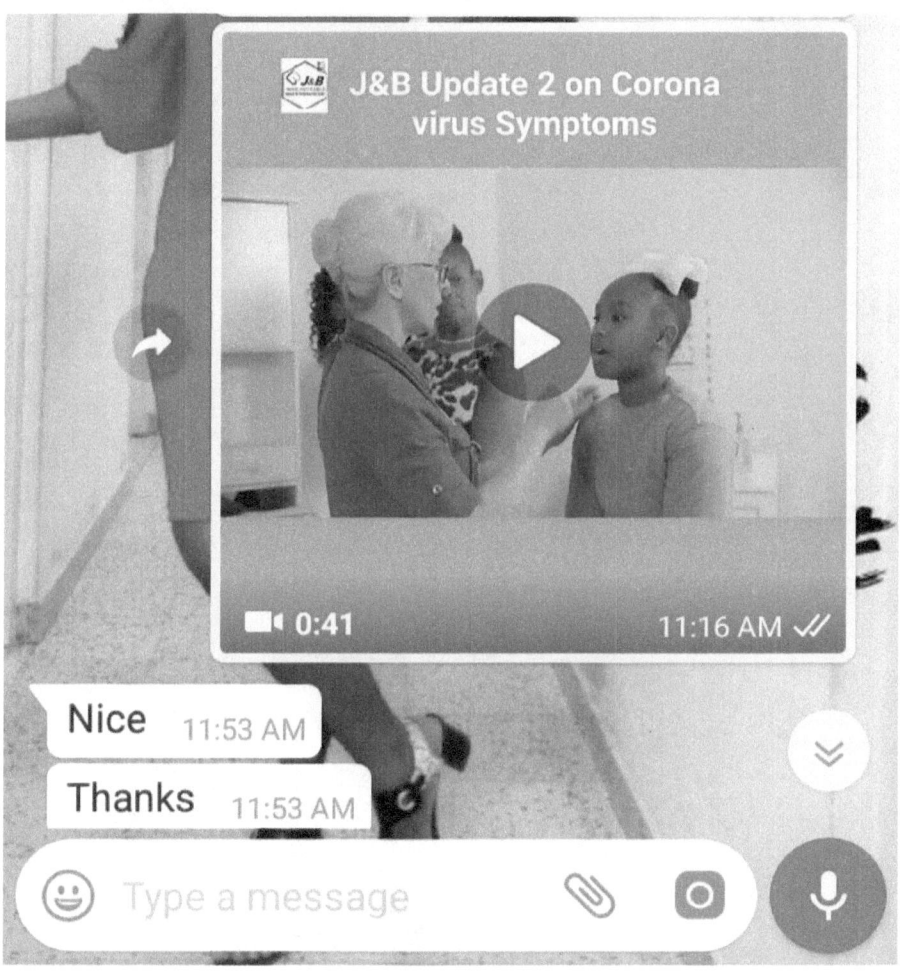

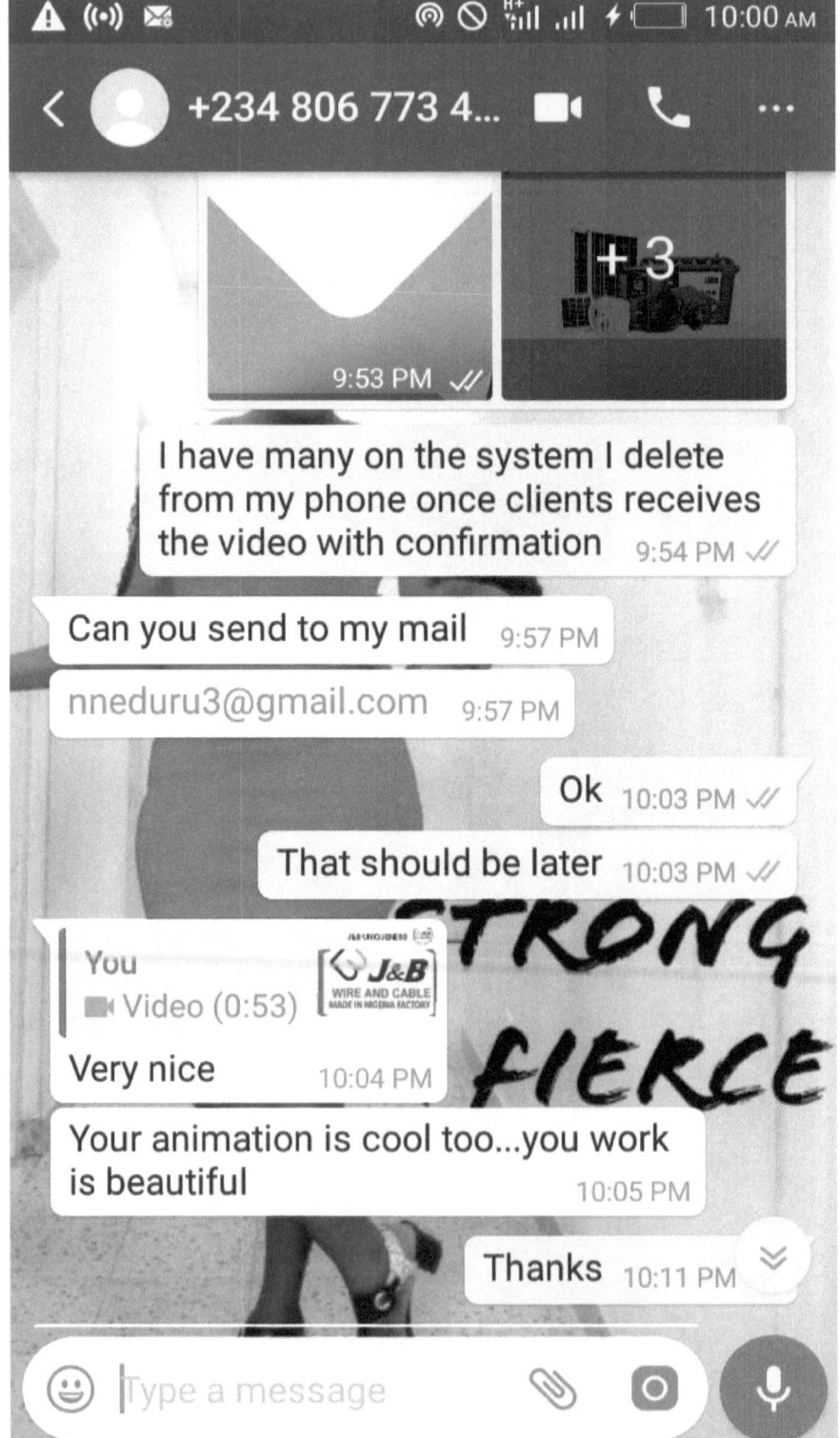

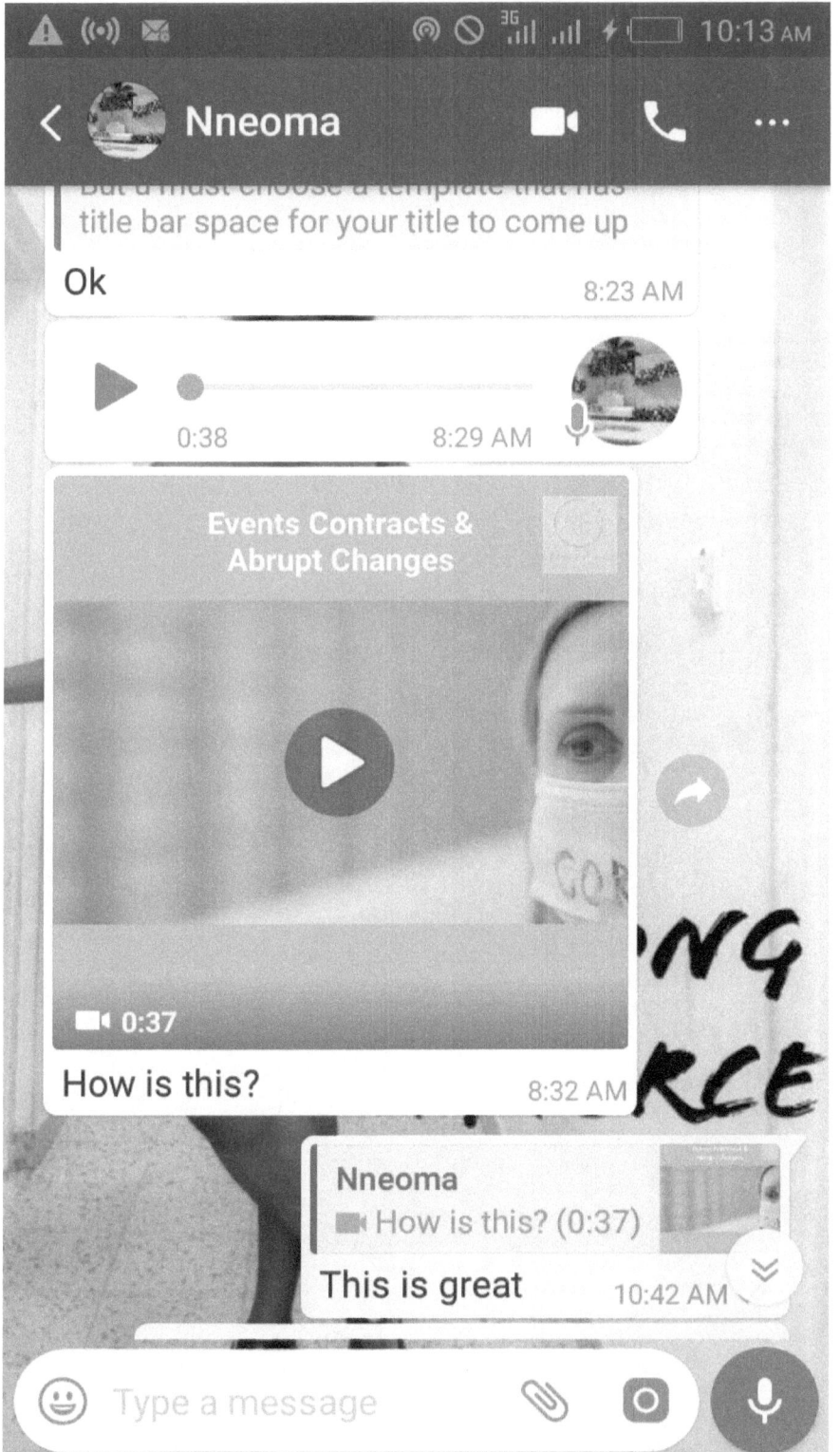

## HOW TO CONTACT THE AUTHOR

Email Address: nemerezion@gmail.com

Phone Number: +2347068021981

Facebook page: Nemere Animator

www.ingramcontent.com/pod-product-compliance
Lightning Source LLC
Chambersburg PA
CBHW031511210526
45463CB00008B/3191